But Who Preside?

A review of Issues concerning 'Lay Presidency' in parts of South America and in the Anglican Communion at large

by
Alan Hargrave

Lay missionary in Bolivia 1981-87, member of the Executive Council of the Province of the Southern Cone, 1982-86
Currently assistant curate, Holy Trinity Church, Cambridge

GROVE BOOKS LIMITED
Bramcote   Nottingham   NG9 3DS

CONTENTS

COMMENDATION

I first met Alan Hargrave in South America in 1985, when I was in the diocese of Chile, which is at the centre of the issue Alan airs here. The story has not really been told in England before, and I am delighted that Grove Books Ltd. can now publish it.

Despite what is said on page 13 below—or perhaps in line with it—no group in the 'Mission and Ministry' Section of Lambeth 1988 was briefed to consider the issue of lay presidency. The Bishop of Chile asked that it should be discussed, and the group tackling liturgy (of which I was secretary) stretched its terms of reference slightly and aired delegated lay presidency as one of three main options for meting a shortage of sacramental ministrations. When the draft came back to the section, there was a move to exclude even a mention of the possibility. On the group, as we re-considered our draft, we thought the reaction of the section was itself significant, and thus re-drafted with a sentence that said that we thought that the issue should at least be discussed. We went back with the new draft to the section in its sub-plenary, and were told to take out even that unthreatening mention. So we did. See the Statement (para.205) and my Commentary in *Lambeth and Liturgy 1988,* page 23.

Curiously, in England there have nevertheless been voices to utter the seemingly unutterable. One such has been the annual Anglican Evangelical Assembly; another has been the passing remarks of the Bishop of Salisbury, John Austin Baker. What Alan Hargrave's account helps to focus is that we need to be clear on what ecclesiological basis such advocacy is made, and within what canonical parameters it is proposed that 'lay presidency' should then be exercised. Whilst he writes out of a sense of urgent necessity in places of pastoral need in the Southern Cone, it is nevertheless principles with which he grapples.

I think we should need to clear away the notion that *if* delegation of the role occurs, then that *is* ordination, whether by post, or FAX, or phone-call! Delegation of this sort, whether it be desirable or not (which is the issue at hand), is proposed exactly to avoid the over-kill of ordination, and we would be wise to keep the two matters distinct.

Indeed, we clearly *could* have delegation, and it *could* be principled and wholly un-anarchic. But perhaps we have only limited time in which actually to address that possibility, before anarchy does come upon us. It would be sad if leadership of the Anglican Churches simply resorted corporately to the stance of the ostrich, and refused to look the challenge in the face. After all, there are either *sound* theological reasons or *no* sound theological reasons why we should not proceed to this style of delegated presidency, and we would surely do better to know which? Sweeping an issue under the carpet is ridiculous.

Colin Buchanan, July 1990

THE COVER PICTURE

is by Peter Ashton, following an idea of the author's

First Impression July 1990

ISSN 0144-1728

ISBN 1 85174 151 8

1. THE ISSUE IN THE
SOUTHERN CONE OF SOUTH AMERICA

Not so quiet on the Western Front

On 3 May 1986, a little publicized event was taking place in Salta, a city in the north of Argentina. Those leaders of the Anglican Church who were aware of what was happening waited with bated breath. The Province of the Southern Cone of South America, the newest Province within the Communion (inaugurated in 1983), was debating this motion:

'The Dioceses of Chile and Peru with Bolivia are authorized to license deacons or lay people to celebrate Holy Communion according to the stipulations laid down in the document "Towards an Apostolic Ministry" . . . for an experimental period of three years.' (The stipulations are explained later.)

There were, in 1986, five dioceses, each represented in the Synod by a bishop, a clergyman and a lay person, and there were present as well a number of observers, including some from other Provinces. After a long and difficult debate the voting, which included that of the Primate, was: seven in favour, eight against. Thus the motion was defeated by a single vote!

Relief echoed through the Anglican Consultative Council (which, according to a letter from Sam Van Culin, had been 'stirred . . . very deeply' by the proposal). What the Archbishop of Canterbury described, in his reply to the proposals, as a 'highly controversial' and 'divisive' issue had been laid to rest, and the Communion could now focus its worries back onto women's ordination. But was it laid to rest, or was this just the first wave of the tide to come?

Anglicans in South America

From the point of view of Anglican Church structures, South America can be divided into three parts: The Southern Cone Province or 'Cono Sur' (including Argentina, Bolivia, Chile, Paraguay, Peru and Uruguay), in which the Lay Presidency debate was focused; Brazil (a Province in its own right); and the remaining northern Republics, which still form part of the Episcopal Church of the USA (from which Brazil gained its independence some years ago).

The Cono Sur has its roots in the UK. First, there are churches established to serve the needs of the British communities (in the major cities, particularly of Argentina) which tend to be conservative with regard to tradition. Secondly, there are churches founded by evangelical missionaries who sought to take the gospel to unevangelized indigenous peoples in Northern Argentina, Paraguay and Southern Chile. Though both are now under the same ecclesiastical umbrella, with evangelism directed largely towards Latins, their distinctive influences are still felt, some dioceses being predominantly influenced by one and some the other.

Added to this, the Anglican church is very small. It is dwarfed not just by the Roman Catholic church, to which about 90% of the population owe at least nominal allegiance, but by other protestant churches (largely evangelical and pentecostal) which are often linked with US fundamentalism. Despite strands of Liberation Theology and the Charismatic movement in the Roman Catholic church, much of it is still pre-Vatican II in its outlook. Hence a strong antagonism between these groups. In the midst of this the tiny Anglican Church strives to take a middle way, stressing its allegiance to *Sola scriptura* whilst attempting to maintain its Anglican heritage with regard to liturgy, ministry and sacraments, adapted to the reality of South America. Two other factors must be mentioned. Not only is the Anglican church small, but it is thinly spread over a vast geographical area. It is also a growing church, committed to mission in all its different aspects.

Thus the diocese of Chile, enjoying rapid church growth but working over long distances with few ordained ministers (most of whom receive the majority of their income from secular employment), began to outline a strategy for ministry aimed at mobilizing the laity, breaking down the sharp division between clergy and lay people, providing ongoing, flexible and practically orientated training (for all its members, including clergy) and including within each congregation adequate provision of 'word and sacrament' (seen as essentially a 'presbyteral' function) as well as 'practical ministries' (seen in terms of a revitalized 'diaconate'). The original study document[1] included two controversial proposals which required a change in the diocesan Canons. The diocese, not wishing to take unilateral action, the document to the Province for its consideration.

The first change (not considered here but a subject of considerable interest and debate within the Anglican Communion) involved the diaconate, to be redefined largely (but not exclusively) in terms of practical ministries, to be seen as a possible permanent calling, and no longer to be used simply as a trial period for the presbyterate. Thus it was proposed that someone preparing for the presbyterate would undergo a considerable period as a licensed 'assistant pastor' but would then be ordained direct to the presbyterate, which involved the first proposed change of canon. This motion was also defeated by a single vote, largely on the grounds that presbyters and bishops must never lose sight of their *diaconia*, and that the proposals could still be implemented even if it meant ordaining deacon and presbyter at the same time (a practice not uncommon now in some Cono Sur dioceses).

The second proposed change was more radical still. Because of the shortage of priests and rapid growth in some areas communion for many congregations had become a very infrequent event, this in a church which is convinced of the centrality of the eucharist to its life ('a congregation is incomplete until it can count on such a ministry'[2]) and which was striving to maintain a balance between Word and Sacrament within the polarization of Catholic and Protestant in Chile. It was therefore proposed that in exceptional circumstances lay people should be licensed by the bishop to preside at Communion.

---

[1] *'El Desarrollo del Ministerio y Estudios Teologicos en la Iglesia Anglicana',* (Dicesis de Chile, 1983).
[2] HUMA (see later) para.6.2.

'(Note: 'lay presidency' is used throughout this report to denote any person who is not a priest/presbyter or bishop presiding at a communion service, without the use of previously consecrated elements. Some may find the term incongruous and prefer, say, 'delegated presidency', an issue discussed later.)

Though the proposals came from Chile, the situation faced by that diocese is common to all the Cono Sur dioceses. For example, I myself, having as a licensed lay preacher, with other lay colleagues, established a small congregation in Santa Cruz, Bolivia's second city, found myself 500 miles by road from the nearest Anglican priest in La Paz. Thus we were only able to celebrate communion on average every 4-6 months, when the bishop (who lived in Lima, Peru, over 1000 miles away) came to visit. On one occasion we were visited by an English clergyman, who, after a half hour practice at reading the Eucharistic prayer in Spanish (a language he did not understand), presided for us at the eucharist (a procedure which I would not, on reflection, repeat). On the other hand I *was* able to preach, lead worship, baptize, bury the dead and conduct weddings, all of which I did.

The ramifications of such a situation go way beyond the lack of provision of communion. A congregation soon begins to infer a very high theology of the eucharist and the ordained ministry (particularly in a traditional RC culture), which there may be no intention of implying. The fact that this one act, and this alone, in the regular life of the local church, is of such significance as to require a special person, someone the congregation may not even know, to perform it, elevates both the event and the performer to almost magical status. Furthermore, it becomes an act divorced from the daily life of the Christian community, almost foreign to it, something from outside rather than something springing from within. This is but one example of many such instances.

The Birth of HUMA

The Chile document was discussed by the Provincial Executive Committee which decided, in view of the importance of the proposals, to produce a summary of the document (leaving out much of the practical detail of training programmes etc.) for circulation to all the other Provinces of the Anglican Communion, inviting their comments.[1] In all, 54 copies were sent out (to some institutions and individuals, mostly evangelicals, as well as to all the Primates) and 27 replies were received, some expressing more than one point of view. The document was also referred to the Cono Sur's own Theological Commission.

In retrospect, the decision to allow individual members of the Executive Committee of the Cono Sur to circulate the document to whomsoever they wished may have been unwise, since it led to a disproportionate response from evangelicals (who, it must be added, were by no means all in favour of the proposals). It does highlight, however, the need for clear guidelines within the Anglican Communion for a consultation procedure between the Provinces on documents of this nature. There is a fear that simply to

[1] *Towards an Apostolic Ministry—'Hacia un Ministerio Apostlico'*—'HUMA' for short.

send a copy to the ACC is insufficient to guarantee a wide enough hearing and response, and may in fact act as a bottleneck through which many important issues fail to pass.

Before considering the comments, it is worth looking in a little more detail at the proposals and the thinking behind them. First of all, both the original Chile document and HUMA were essentially concrete attempts to tackle real and pressings needs. They were pragmatic, rather than well argued theologically. The major theological justification for the changes was stated as 'applying the Biblical concept of the *Priesthood of All Believers* to the situation in our Dioceses'.[1] This concept was never developed, but simply stated as though it were commonly understood and accepted. 'The priesthood of all believers was defined at the time of the Reformation but never developed fully in practice, leaving an inadequate concept of ministry in the church'.[2]

Secondly, there was no open-ended time-scale. HUMA was circulated in December 1984 and replies were sought by March 1985 (a number of recipients complained about the limited time-scale). Furthermore, it was sent before the Cono Sur's own Theological Commission had had the chance to consider the document and report back. Thus there was no opportunity to modify HUMA in the light of their findings. The reasons for this were twofold. First of all, (largely for economic reasons) the Provincial Executive only met every six months and the Provincial Synod every three years (it was due to meet in May '86). Hence, rapid reviews were impossible. Secondly, the dioceses supporting the motion (Chile with the backing of Peru/Bolivia) were keen (and indeed under grass roots pressure) to implement the proposals as soon as possible to give time for at least two years of experimentation prior to Lambeth, '88, where the issue could then be reflected upon in the light of 'praxis' (very much 'liberation theology' style, though Chile diocese would by no means identify itself as such).

Thirdly, although it would obviously have been impractical to translate and send the whole of the original document (some 45 pages), HUMA inevitably lost, in its brevity (5 pages), something of the context of the overall proposals, of which the specific points relating to 'ordination direct to an order' and 'lay presidency' were just a small part. HUMA sees lay presidency as exceptional, rather than normative. 'It is normal in the church for the Sacraments of Baptism and Holy Communion to be celebrated by those who have been duly ordained priest by an Anglican Bishop'[3] (note that Baptism and Communion are treated together in this context) and 'we are here talking about exceptional cases'.[4] Thus the long-term solution: 'it is desired that each congregation should have its own priest as soon as possible'.[5] This is worth bearing in mind, since, as we shall see later, not all those favouring Lay Presidency would view it as exceptional, including some in the Cono Sur.

[1] HUMA paras.1.2 and 8.2.2(c).
[2] *Ibid.* para.8.1.2.
[3] *Ibid.* para.6.1.
[4] *Ibid.* para.8.2.3.
[5] *Ibid.* para.6.2.

With this in mind the conditions for Lay Presidency were closely defined.[1] The person concerned should:

  i. Be given an episcopal licence, valid only for two years (or until the person were ordained priest, or a priest were appointed), renewable at the Bishop's discretion.
  ii. Be a mature Christian *man* (women's ordination was not an issue in the Cono Sur at that time).
  iii. Be approved by the Church Council.
  iv. Receive any preparation required by the Bishop.
  v. Have already been involved in the ministry 'area' of 'Word and Sacraments' (as opposed to the area of 'Practical Ministries').[2]

In addition the licence was only to operate in one congregation, and if a priest or Bishop were visiting, he would preside.

A further proviso was later added at the recommendation of the Theological Commission—that the person be a member of the Anglican Church (!) and that preference be given to a deacon, if there were one in the congregation.

Finally, the whole proposal was to be for an experimental period of just three years.

Alternatives to Lay Presidency

What does not come over strongly in HUMA is the fact that people in the Province had struggled with this problem for many years and had indeed considered and practised a number of alternatives.

i. Itinerant priests travelling around remote congregations to provide communion. This has been (and still is) the practice in many areas in the Cono Sur. However, as already stated, it tends to imply an elevated theology of eucharist and ordained ministry. It also means that communion is infrequently celebrated in many congregations, which cuts against recent ecumenical agreement. (e.g. 'The Eucharist should be celebrated frequently'[3] and 'we believe that (weekly eucharist) should be accepted as the norm'[4]). Furthermore, there is the danger of separating presidency of the eucharist from presiding over the life of the congregation (cf ARCIC 'It is right that he who has oversight in the church and is the focus of its unity should preside at ... the Eucharist').[5] In many such congregations leadership exists which carries the responsibility for every aspect of church life yet does not have the authority to celebrate communion. (This is true in many churches in the UK in rural areas or during interregnums.) Thus there is a separation between authority and responsibility which seems impossible to justify theologically. (It is worth noting that the original proposals some years ago for 'Regional Episcopacy', now widely accepted, based their argument on just this point, that you cannot exercise authority without responsibility, and came from the same source—

[1] *Ibid.* paras.6.5–6.7.
[2] *Ibid.* paras.3 and 4.
[3] *Baptism Eucharist and Ministry* (WCC, 1982) p.16 para.30.
[4] *God's Reign and Our Unity* (SPCK, 1984) p.45 para.71.
[5] ARCIC, *Final Report* (SPCK, 1982) p.35 para.12.

the diocese of Chile!) ARCIC cites Ignatius: 'The man exercising this oversight presided at the Eucharist and no other could do so without his consent'.[1] Though ARCIC does not interpret it in this way, it almost seems to offer a mandate for lay presidency, with the bishop's consent!

In favour of the 'travelling priest' approach is the argument that whoever presides must represent not just the local church but the universal church, and because ordination, potentially at least, is to the universal church, it provides the only acceptable focus of unity.[2] However, baptism is also into the universal, not the local church, yet there is widespread agreement in the Anglican Communion that a deacon or even a lay person may administer baptism—even someone with no recognized office in the church, such as a midwife. It is difficult to maintain this line of argument for communion unless it is strictly maintained for baptism as well. Note that, for deacons at least, it is not just exceptional, but normal practice, for them to baptize.

ii. A number of Provinces favour the use of the reserved sacrament.[3] This is rejected by Chile and the other dioceses in the Cono Sur which stand in the evangelical tradition.[4] At stake is the question: in what way is Christ present at the Eucharist? This of course was a major issue at the time of the Reformation, in reaction to the adoration of 'the 'Host', and related practices. Neill suggests that Cranmer: 'desired to exclude absolutely the idea that the presence of Christ in the Eucharist is a local presence' and adds 'consecration and communion were to become a single act'.[5]

There is a degree of ambivalence on this point in modern ecumenical thinking regarding the eucharist. ARCIC implies that Christ's presence is not limited to the elements[6] but then seems to contradict itself in the same section: 'Before the eucharistic prayer, to the question: "what is that?" the believer answers: "it is bread". After . . . he answers: "it is the body of Christ".' Thus ARCIC justifies 'extension' of communion 'to those unable to attend', which has fairly wide, though not universal support[7], as well as allowing for 'adoration of Christ in the reserved sacrament'[8]—a practice unacceptable to most protestants.

Linked with the move away from the notion of a precise 'moment' of consecration is the appreciation of communion as a total act, which does not end with the blessing: 'Christ fulfils the Eucharist in his people when the communicants go into the world . . . as witnesses of the Kingdom of God'.[9] Extending communion to the sick following a eucharistic celebration does not appear at odds with this principle.

[1] ARCIC op.cit. p.35 para.12.
[2] eg. BEM op. cit. p.16 para.29.
[3] See ACC 7, p.57 and Lambeth Conference 1988 Proceedings p.73.
[4] HUMA para.8.2.5.
[5] S. Neill, Anglicanism (Mowbrays, 1977) pp.72f.
[6] ARCIC op. cit. p.21 para.6.
[7] Cf. BEM p.16 para.32.
[8] Op. cit. p.23 para.8.
[9] God's Reign and Our Unity p.40 para.63.

However, reservation for the purpose of adoration of Christ in the sacrament or for transfer outside the normal eucharistic fellowship seems to move far beyond the concept of consecration and communion as a single act. 'This is an unreformed practice which strikes at the root of all that a celebration of communion is meant to be', says the Bishop of Manchester in a letter to the *Church Times* (19 Oct. 1984).

Yet again we are in the area of inferred theology. If the sacrament is reserved, what does this imply about the presence of Christ? Despite much progress in our understanding of *anamnesis*, it surely gives the elements a mystical (if not magical) significance we may not wish to imply and suggests a mechanical conveyancing of grace independent of the whole eucharistic act, which must include right reception (cf. 1 Cor. 11.27ff) and eucharistic living (cf. Rom. 12.1 and note the comments of the Quakers and Salvation Army in reply to BEM).[1] There appears to be something of an ecumenical 'fudge factor' operative on this point in a number of texts, the only solution to which would be to hold together consecration and reception as a single act, both conceptually and in time (another point stressed by the Bishop of Manchester in his letter to the *Church Times*, mentioned above.)

iii. The practice which receives widest support is that of ordaining local priests. One wonders, reading some of the replies to HUMA, whether people have properly understood the document, for that is central to its purpose. In fact the Cono Sur has been at the forefront of this move, particularly in the past two decades. The vast majority of the priests in the Province are non-stipendiary (a reflection of the stark economic realities). Many would be considered ill-equipped for the ordained ministry in other areas, educationally at least. Not one of the presbyters among the indigenous people of Northern Argentina has secondary school education—not even the bishop! Training programmes by extension were developed (many of which have now been translated into other languages, including English), to enable people to study and work at the same time (these were fully outlined in the original Chile Document). So the Province can hardly be accused of reserve in this area, particularly when compared to 'First World' Anglicans. Why then do the dioceses involved not simply ordain more priests?

It is difficult for the church in the UK to imagine a situation where new congregations are constantly being formed, as, for example, where the relatively new diocese of Peru with Bolivia grew from just one congregation to over 20 in 12 years. Even where growth is taking place in the Church of England, it is generally within the framework of an existing congregation which includes people who have been Christians for a number of years, have received considerable instruction in the faith and shown maturity of discipleship over a long period of time. In new congregations, particularly in more remote areas, this may not be the case at all. Our own experience in Bolivia was of seeing a congregation grow rapidly to fifty or so people, yet none had been Christians more than two years. This does

[1] M Thurian *Ecumenical Perspectives on BEM* (WCC, 1983), p.161f.

not exclude opportunity for growth in discipleship and the taking of responsibility in the life of the church, but experience shows that it is not generally sufficient time to prove a person's call to the ordained ministry, which implies lifelong commitment.

There have been a number of tragic examples in the Cono Sur of men ordained because of the urgency to provide priests, who later abandoned their 'irrevocable' calling, causing great damage to the church. Some have even used their letters of orders as a basis for financial exploitation. It is in this context that HUMA section 6.3 states 'hands ought not to be laid on a person without adequate preparation and testing of his calling'.[1] Drawing, perhaps, from his experience of a similar context, Archbishop Russell of Cape Town, in his reply to HUMA, declared:'If I were asked to choose between the proliferation of persons ordained priest so that Holy Eucharist may be celebrated and the granting of a licence to lay persons which must certainly be regarded as withdrawable, then my vote would lie in the direction of the second'. As HUMA rightly states: 'much more is involved in priesthood than celebrating Holy Communion'.[2]

Thus HUMA proposed lay presidency, as an exception and largely for pragmatic reasons. However, in its desire for urgent implementation of the proposals, it sacrificed both a fully reasoned appeal to its context (which is not properly explained, even in the original Chile document) and, even more importantly, a persuasive theological justification of its conclusions.

The Provincial Theological Commission

Perhaps the most important response to HUMA was from its own Theological Commission, since its members were fully conversant with the background to the report and the local situation. A meeting was called and took place over six days in January 1985, to see if there were theological objections to the proposed changes of canon. In the mean-time, the Commission's co-ordinator, John Cobb, wrote to the Provincial Council with some reflections of his own. He noted that there were no simple yes/no type answers to such a question, since it raised a host of other issues concerning ministry in general, Holy Orders in particular and the nature of the eucharist. He also pointed out a fundamental problem with the HUMA document, which was later picked up in a number of replies, which was its lack of a coherent basis ('un hilo conductor') for its arguments. For example, the bland acceptance of the threefold order in HUMA 2.3 seems to contradict the desire to return to 'the position of the New Testament church'. Also in 8.2.2(b) the 39 Articles are rejected as applying to a 'different religious context', whereas they are appealed to for support in 8.2.3.

The implication in HUMA that there is a consensus concerning the mean-ing of Holy Orders is also challenged. 'Some by definition see a presbyter as one equipped to preside at Holy Communion' says Cobb. The same applies to the understanding of 'consecration'. More importantly, the

[1] Cf. J. Tiller *A Strategy for the Church's Ministry* (CIO, 1983) p.122.
[2] *Op. cit.* para.8.2.4.

point is made (which HUMA seems to ignore) that there is no consensus about theological method in the Anglican Communion, particularly concerning use of Scripture. The Bible does not provide for us a set of 'prefabricated structures'.

This is of particular importance in the light of current New Testament studies of ministry. Traditional use of Scripture to prove the three-fold ministry has been largely discredited.[1] Moberley, writing almost a century ago in defence of the presbyter as sole celebrant of Holy Communion, states confidently 'if it were not implicit as part of the leadership of the presbyteral office, then we must needs have good evidence of the existence of some other distinct and higher stratum in the spiritual order for the breaking of bread'.[2] Note the assumption of a hierarchical system. This would appear more to reflect sociological factors in Victorian England than biblical principles of ministry.

The point is taken up by Roland Allen, who only in recent years has received the attention he deserves for his visionary writings. Arguing in 1922 for the ordination of local men in the local church, he particularly attacks the likes of Bishop King, General Secretary of SPG, who wrote: 'he (the missionary) has let the reins of power pass from his hands and can only advise and exhort where he ought to rule'[3] (paradoxically, Allen's book was published by 'World Dominion Press'!).

Allen's misgivings are born out by scholars such as Schweizer who finds 'both free and fixed forms' of church order in the New Testament.[4] Kruse finds in St Paul a 'situationist response' to different contexts, leading to different styles of ministry operative within a framework of apostleship, servanthood and the power of the Holy Spirit.[5] Dunn concludes that the NT does not provide a single model but the basis for a multiplicity of structures, only later developing into the three-fold ordained ministry due to a change of eschatological perspective.[6] It is even acknowledged in ecumenical discussions: 'all attempts to read off one divinely authorized form of ministry from the New Testament are futile'.[7]

The New Testament certainly offers little help as to who should preside at the eucharist.[8] The case has even been made for the whole congregation saying the Eucharistic prayer. This seems to follow easily from the Anglican/Reformed statement: '*The church* prays to the Father for the gift of the Holy Spirit in order that the Eucharistic event may be a reality'.[9] This is important since if, as seems likely, there is growing mutual recognition

[1] Cf. S. Sykes and J. Booty (eds.) *The Study Of Anglicanism* (SPCK 1988) p.292.
[2] R. Moberley *Ministerial Priesthood* (Murray, 1899) p.267.
[3] R. Allen *Spontaneous Expansion of the Church* (1927) p.180.
[4] E Schweizer *Church Order in the New Testament* (SCM, 1961) p.225.
[5] C. Kruse *New Testament Foundations of Ministry* (MMS, 1983) pp.177-184.
[6] J. Dunn *Unity and Diversity in the New Testament* (SCM, 1977) p.122 and pp.341ff.
[7] *God's Reign* and *Our Unity op. cit.* p.49 para.77.
[8] L. Boff *Ecclesiogenesis* (Collins, 1986) p.64; T. Lloyd (Grove Liturgical Study no. 9, 1977) p.30.
[9] *God's Reign and Our Unity op. cit.* para.60.

of ministries between denominations, it will be a recognition of diversity, not of uniformity.

The Theological Commission itself pointed to a number of other issues, in particular the need to describe more clearly the South American context, especially the role, and often elitist status, of clergy in popular religion and the danger, by hastily ordaining priests, of producing second-class presbyters reduced to a cultic function. They also added extra safeguards to the proposals (mentioned above) and repeated some of the points already made by Cobb. They were not able to reach a consensus, however, on the specific proposals. As Cobb commented: 'there are divergencies of opinion between members of the Commission', which seemed to reflect the traditions of their parent dioceses.

What is unfortunately apparent is that, with more time for reflection, the Province could have taken on board the vital comments of their own Commission and produced a much more coherent version of HUMA before circulating it to the other Provinces. Their haste probably greatly contributed to the defeat of the proposals.

The Replies
The replies to HUMA were analyzed by the Provincial Theological Commission and by the Church in Wales for the Toronto Primates meeting in 1986. There was a good deal of admiration of the Province for its dynamic attempt to meet the needs of growth. It is interesting to note that the churchmanship of the authors does not seem to be reflected in any systematic way in their replies.

The central HUMA concept of 'priesthood of all believers' was dismissed as at best 'confusing, as the authors' understanding of it . . . is never made clear' or at worst 'a source of controversy' (Bishop of N. Queensland) and 'irrelevant' (Roger Beckwith, Latimer House). This highlights the danger, particularly when a document is intended for a wide audience, of failing to define terms.

The problem of lack of priests was evident in a number of areas: eg. 'in Guyana we have 160 congregations and 30 priests' (Goodrich, West Indies). However, the majority were not in favour of lay presidency, preferring either to ordain more local priests or else to use the reserved sacrament. Several replies highlighted the problem of 'indelibility' of orders. Some of the replies smacked of paternalism: 'this new Province needs to be guided'. The strength of opposition to the proposals from the USA was surprising given their own unilateral action on women's ordination—though it may reflect that church's own need for symbols of historic continuity as a small communion in a country where many denominations have severed links with ancient patterns. Many, including the Archbishop of Canterbury, felt that the issue should be raised at ACC-7 and Lambeth, irrespective of the outcome of the Cono Sur vote.

What is most notable is the lack of well-argued theological objection to the proposals (which may also reflect a lack of time available). If it is true that the original document lacked theological cohesion, the same can be said of most of the replies. The major arguments against the proposals were on the grounds of tradition: 'Lay celebration...cuts at the root of Anglican formularies, practice and history, and would isolate us from our whole catholic tradition' (Archbishop of Dublin) or on the grounds of unity: 'it would certainly be highly divisive within the Church of England and the rest of the Communion' (Prov of Australia) (divisive, added others, such as Archbishop McAdoo, within ecumenical endeavours, too).

Corridors of Power

It is worth tracing the debate on lay presidency within the ACC. At ACC-6 in 1984, the council favoured 'the ordination of local priests to meet the need' but went on 'We commend the subject for further discussion at ACC-7 and Lambeth '88' (p.67). At ACC-7, 1987, there was a change in emphasis: 'a lay person *cannot* preside in the commonly understood sense of consecrating the elements' (hence the exception taken to the term 'lay presidency'). There seemed to be a shift towards favouring use of the reserved sacrament, with examples cited from Brazil and New Zealand. However, a number of serious questions were recommended to the churches for discussion, such as: the status of the congregation in the context of the Eucharistic prayer and the use of the words of institution by a lay person.

The report from Lambeth '88, however, fails to mention lay presidency and speaks only of the ordination of local people and use of the reserved sacrament. There is no mention of HUMA in ACC-7 or Lambeth '88. More importantly, there is no theological justification either for rejection of lay presidency or for use of the reserved sacrament, or for the shift in stance in the ACC. The only rationale seems defence of the *status quo*, a premise expressly rejected in the Anglican/Reformed dialogue on ministry: 'Not all the developments of the past nineteen centuries are to be regarded as divinely sanctioned simply because they have occurred'.[1]

At the Synod of the Cono Sur when the crucial vote was taken, delegates were deeply influenced by the call to avoid division in the church and to wait for ACC-7 and Lambeth where the issue would be debated by the wider Communion. Others, more sceptical, feared that unless the proposals were accepted and the lay presidency experiment initiated, they would never be dealt with at all at Lambeth. History proved them right, leaving many people in the Cono Sur feeling disillusioned, and even deceived, by unfulfilled promises. For some, South America appeared to be the victim not just of political and economic, but of ecclesiastical imperialism as well. Their cause seemed well and truly lost.

---

[1] *God's Reign and Our Unity op. cit.* para.77.

2. A WORLDWIDE ISSUE

Not Alone

In 1977 Lloyd, in the preface to a Grove booklet on lay presidency states: 'Lay presidency is not yet a hotly debated issue through the length and breadth of the Anglican countryside, but it will be as the increasingly confused debate over the nature of ordination is brought sharply to a head by the continuing fall in numbers of men in the ordained ministry'. But the issue is not confined to the United Kingdom and South America.

Roland Allen, reflecting upon Scripture in the light of his own experience of Communion at home with his family, points to its relationship to the Passover, which is essentially a 'family rite' rather than a 'temple rite'.[1] He advocates knowledge gained from innovative practice reflected upon for a long time and in different places. Thus he greatly prefers the model of family communion, defined essentially by the *relationships* of the participants rather than structures and formularies, which make for 'an individualistic act'. Rather than destroy the universality of the event, he feels it upholds it, since it creates a model which provides a richer vision for the universal. Note his emphasis on ecclesiology. His primary focus is the community of believers, not the minister. The fact that he was ordained priest seemed to him irrelevant. It was, for him, his natural status as head of the household which gave him the right to preside. 'I was doing what I wished all Christian heads of households to do'. He goes on to argue that there is no essential difference between baptism and eucharist and suggests that if a deacon or lay person can baptize, he should also celebrate communion. Allen was from a high church background but his use of Scripture and methodology seem to align him with liberation theologians of today.

Further support for lay presidency comes from an unexpected source. William Temple, in his address to the Manchester Diocesan Conference in 1928, states: We must, I believe, come to the conclusion that . . . any layman who should devoutly and not defiantly decide that it is right for him to celebrate the Holy Communion would effect a real consecration and through it the real gift would be given. There is nothing, so to speak, in the nature of things which makes it impossible for any but priests to celebrate and administer a real sacrament'.[2]

In more recent times the issue was brought to the fore in the Anglican Congress of 1963 by Canon F. Synge of New Zealand, another High Churchman. Asking if the ministry in the church were structurally fitted for its changing task, he suggested that one of the greatest obstacles was the entrenchment of the clergy in a position of privilege and of professional indispensability (something which merits serious evaluation). Arguing for lay presidency in exceptional cases (cf. Allen, who seems to argue for it to be normative) he begins not with the community (cf. Allen again) but with the bishop. 'Every Eucharist is a Bishop's Eucharist', his authority to preside being delegated to his presbyters.[3] (The issue has been debated widely at ground level in New Zealand and Australia in the last decade).

[1] D. Paton, *Reform of the Ministry* (Lutterworth, 1968) p.201f.
[2] Quoted in the *Church of England Newspaper* (1 October, 1982) p.7.
[3] F. Synge in *Proceedings of the Anglican Congress* (Toronto, 1963) p.159.

He sees the Eucharist as the Christian community's offering for all those in its care, a work greatly hindered by lack of priests, which 'stems from an insufficiently high doctrine of the church and an unwarrantably high doctrine of the presbyterate'.[1] If the Bishop can delegate his authority to presbyters (lifelong delegation), why not to lay people (temporary delegation)?. However, in arguing his case he seems to elevate episcopacy to unprecedented proportions. His thesis did not gain wide support. Perhaps the most searching question came from the then Bishop of London: 'What is the difference between delegation and ordination, and is not ordination the official delegation of Episcopal authority?'. This is a question to which we must return.

The issue 'attained the status of a long running saga' in the 1970's at St John's Theological College, Nottingham, from which Lloyd's Grove booklet seemed to stem. There was a definite swing away from 'exceptional circumstances', such as an interregnum, to arguing for lay presidency in a variety of situations, including tutorial groups (some of which were led by ordained ministers, some by lay tutors), home groups, occasional groups such as at conferences, the sick and housebound, and where there is only one minister for several centres of worship. Points about lack of New Testament evidence for presidency at communion and the delegation of the bishop's authority were again mentioned, together with an affirmation that 'matters of order' (referring to the ordained ministry) 'are secondary to matters of doctrine', particularly in the light of 'much new understanding of the church as the people of God'[2], which seems to echo Allen's experience (above).

The point being made is that the ordained ministry, as it operates within Anglicanism, is not of the essence of the church, whereas the eucharist is. Thus Lloyd asks what is the eucharistic community, and wonders why it is OK to celebrate communion in almost any situation (eg. clergy chapters) providing there is a priest present, whereas a parish church meeting on a Sunday without a priest cannot celebrate communion.

By contrast, Moltmann argues against the idea of 'the Lord's Supper' as a closed shop, open only to the tried and tested faithful. He sees it as a 'feast open to the churches' (i.e. denominations) and 'to the world', thereby demonstrating the community's catholicity and its mission. In line with this he also appears to have no objection to lay presidency, drawing strongly on the example of charismatic communities of the New Testament: 'The celebration ... is not bound to any particular ministry, though it is bound to the "ministry" in the sense of the calling and mission of the whole congregation and every individual .. '.[3]

The *Theology of Ordination* report to the General Synod (GS 281) in 1975 defended the traditional Anglican position, greatly stressing the need for 'universality' of which the priest is a focus. Lay presidency was rejected on the grounds of it being 'a cause of division' (p.20). However, though not front page news, lay presidency had definitely emerged as an important issue in the Church of England.

[1] *Ibid.* p.160.
[2] St John's College Council Meeting, Item 6, p.3, 21 May 1976.
[3] J. Moltmann *The Church in the Power of the Spirit* (SCM, 1977) p.260.

More recently the Tiller report discusses lay presidency, but points to the fact that the lack of priests in the church is not a temporary emergency but a long-term problem which can only be met by ordaining local priests. Tiller judges that it would be necessary to establish 'in principle' that lay leaders should have authority to preside at the eucharist, and wants to know 'how one would distinguish theologically between the recognition of that authority and ordination?'.[1] The issue was not raised, however, in the recent BMU report (GS 694) on *The Priesthood of The Ordained Ministry*, though, in line with recent scholarship, they admit that 'no priesthood is attributed to the distinctive ministry in the New Testament' (p.28).

Card, in a recent work makes the same point and says 'what is fundamentally at issue is the presupposed link between priesthood or the ordained ministry and the eucharist'.[2] It may be that such a link should remain, but it demands a more solid theological defence than it has received of late. One almost senses a fear amongst some clergy (though it is rarely expressed) that if this last exclusive function of their priesthood were lost, the priest would be dispensable.

One of the arguments against lay presidency has been on the grounds of problems in the ecumenical dialogue. However, whilst such a move would be currently unacceptable to the Roman Catholic and Orthodox hierarchies, it would put Anglicans in line with some other traditions. For example, the United Reformed Church allows lay presidency in situations of 'pastoral necessity' according to stipulations very similar to those proposed in HUMA, except that the District Council acts in place of the bishop and there is no objection on grounds of sex. A review of the practice found it to work satisfactorily and did not recommend changes, though it noted that there had been some unauthorized celebrations[3] (which certainly occur within the Anglican Communion anyway). A similar situation exists in the Methodist Church, where dispensation is given by Conference and is regarded as 'temporary ordination', though there is no laying on of hands.[4]

However, perhaps the strongest proponents of lay presidency, from a theological point of view at least, come from amongst Roman Catholics. This may well be because their shortage of priests, not helped by the requirement of celibacy, has reached dire proportions. Boff estimates that in Brazil there are 1.8 priests for every 10,000 faithful! Schillebeeckx notes that lay presidency was allowed in exceptional circumstances by Tertullian. His argument centres around the fact that 'the ancient . . . and the modern church cannot envisage any Christian community without the celebration of the eucharist', pointing to the 'essential link between ecclesia and eucharist'.[5] He is convinced that the 'so-called shortage of priests' exists because of a wrong ecclesiology and view of ministry. 'People belong to the universal church because

---

[1] *Op. cit.* p.120; cf. Bishop of London, above.
[2] T. Card, *Priesthood In Crisis* (SCM, 1988) p.105.
[3] URC *Church Life report to the General Assembly* (1980) pp.39-42.
[4] I. Jones, Principal, Wesley House, Personal Communication, 5 May 1989.
[5] E. Schillebeeckx *Ministry* (SCM, 1981) p.72 (cf Kung, below, p.24).

they belong to the local community' which exists 'in solidarity' with other communities, not because they belong to a hierarchical structure, about which, he claims, there is a growing ecumenical consensus.[1]

Kung also wants to begin at the local level. He sees ordination as 'a mandate from the community and its leaders'[2] and would allow for special 'urgent cases' and 'spontaneous charism' leading to 'the possible validity of a eucharistic celebration even without a priest', for example in China or South America.[3] He, like many others, challenges the concept of an 'irreversible . . . indelible character' associated with priesthood.[4]

Perhaps most persuasive is Boff, for he writes out of the dynamic experience of vibrant basic communities in Brazil, where many celebrations of the 'Lord's Supper' already take place, presided over by lay community leaders for want of priests. They ask: 'what is the theological value of our celebrations?'.[5] He relates it to the parallel question for Catholics: what is the value of Protestant celebrations?. His answer focuses again on the question of ecclesiology, a rich and important area for reflection which can only be touched upon here.

Looking at both the New Testament and Church history, he is not alone in noting the bond between presidency of community and presidency of the eucharist. 'The basic rule in ancient Christianity was: whoever presides over the community, be his title bishop, presbyter, prophet, leader or confessor, presides *ex officio* at the eucharist as well'. Furthermore, the celebration is not that of the celebrant alone but of the whole community, which has an 'inalienable right to celebrate the eucharist'.[6] The president of the community is also involved in preaching, admonition, upbuilding, and direction, being selected by the community and accepted by other communities and the bishop. He sees this pattern as normative in the first millenium until the growth of canon law, authority without connection to the community and the creation of clergy benefices, amongst other factors, led to a privatized, ontological ecclesiology.

Boff affirms that apostolic succession is about keeping the apostolic faith, not about laying on of hands. Thus he accepts the validity of protestant church eucharist and ministry. (cf The Papal Bull of 1896: 'Ordinations carried out according to the Anglican rite have been and are absolutely null and utterly void').

But what, he asks, if the extraordinary (as in Brazil) becomes the norm? In that case the church must change its ecclesiology to one based on communion, not power. (Theoretically, at least, this is the case in the Anglican 'Communion', but we have a long way to go before it becomes a reality, even at an inter-Provincial level.) Thus Boff's ecclesiology starts with the

[1] *Ibid.* p.73.
[2] H. Kung *Why Priests?* (Fontana, 1972) p.67 (cf. Schillebeeckx, p.51).
[3] *Ibid* p.35.
[4] *Ibid* p.46f.
[5] L Boff *op. cit.* p. 62.
[6] *Ibid* pp.65, 66.

'faith community', not 'powers transmitted'.[1] The point of reference is not 'to the past via linear succession', but to the 'Risen One', alive today in the community, from which the ordained ministry springs. Thus, he argues that lay coordinators in Brazil are celebrants of a true eucharist, though he later appears to qualify this, perhaps looking over his shoulder at the authorities in Rome. Indeed, as Card reminds us, 'Kung...has had his licence to teach at Catholic Universities withdrawn and Schillebeeckx and Boff . . . have been under investigation'.[2] Such views will probably not prevail, under the present Pope at least, but it is unlikely that they will disappear either. The crisis of ministry cannot go on being shelved.

It is worth asking, if those proposing lay presidency are not linked by churchmanship or theological persuasion, is there any bond that unites them? Perhaps it is their experience on the frontiers of mission and their definition of the theological task, which Boff describes as 'seeking out adequate answers to new and urgent problems'. 'The deposit of faith' he says, is not 'a stagnant cistern' but 'springs of living water'.[3]

So, though the diocese of Chile may have suffered a defeat for their proposals, they may rest assured that the same battle is being waged on many fronts and they are by no means fighting alone. As Buchanan states, 'it is an issue which demands a satisfying theological answer'.[4]

The Central Issues
It would appear that there are two central issues at stake in the debate, which are common to the whole church, and a third, which is a specific issue for Anglicans. The first two centre around the questions: what is ordination? and: what constitutes the church? (both of which have implications for our understanding of the Eucharist). The third issue concerns theological method.

The Ordained Ministry
What was it that the diocese of Chile meant in referring to 'the priesthood of all believers'? The following is an attempt to enter into their thinking.

The early church confronted serious problems. Now that the 'parousia' did not seem so imminent, how should the church organize its life to face, perhaps, a long term future? How could the church maintain unity with so many different and geographically remote communities? What should be done about false teachers who seemed to be leading the church away from the teaching of Christ and the apostles? It is against this background that a universal pattern of leadership, the three fold ordained ministry, began to emerge as an essentially pragmatic solution to ensure order, sound teaching, mission and the preservation of unity in the church.

Along with this, elaborate liturgical worship began to develop, no doubt in part, at least, to preserve sound teaching by agreed formularies in the cult. By the third century, particularly through Cyprian, the 'previously strictly

[1] *Ibid*, p.71.
[2] *Op. cit.* p.27.
[3] *Op. cit.* p.27.
[4] In Lloyd *op. cit.* p.19.

avoided titles' of 'priest' and 'high priest' were being used for the president of the Eucharist, which itself became increasingly thought of in present sacrificial terms.[1] Hanson suggests that it became 'necessary and appropriate to express the priestly ministry . . . of Christ', though he does not justify such a sweeping remark.[2] BEM (p.23) states that 'priest' used at the eucharist does not refer to an Old Testament type priesthood, nor to the priesthood of Christ nor to the priesthood of all believers. However, we find no other sort of priesthood in the New Testament.

Eastwood[3] points to the consequences. A priestly race becomes a priestly class. Spiritual sacrifice becomes priestly sacrifice. A hierarchy develops and, by the middle ages, the term xxxx, used of the whole people of God in the New Testament, becomes a term for 'non-qualified' Christians, having 'virtually . . . no priestly or ministerial function at all'.[4] Note that coupled with the Eucharistic celebration was the 'priestly' function of absolution, which effectively limited not just who performed the rite, but who had access to its benefits. The church, says Hanson, 'placed priesthood between man and God in exclusive possession of the access to the means of grace'[5]; and so the priesthood of all believers was effectively 'abolished'.

The practical rediscovery of the priesthood of all believers was central to the Reformation. Eastwood suggests that for Luther it 'underlies the whole of his teaching'.[1] Note his famous phrase 'every shoemaker can be a priest of God'. Calvin emphasized its dependence on and derivation from Christ's priesthood.[6] It was no good knocking the medieval priesthood in the name of the 'Priesthood of all Believers'. It was first necessary to establish the priesthood of Christ, in which all are invited to share.

However, in practice, the educated ministers still did 'nearly all the ministry', 'a sociological feature of bourgeois Christianity'.[8] (We might reflect on the effect of centuries of Oxbridge graduates as clergy in the Church of England!) The English Reformers, whilst deeply influenced by their continental counterparts, chose to retain the word 'priest' (as etymologically derived from *presbuteros* rather than *sacerdos* or *hiereus*.[9] The BMU suggests that it is not the word itself but 'what the presbyter or bishop does in relation to particular sacramental actions' which is the key issue.[10] But Kung disagrees and desires a terminology not open to misinterpretation.

Vatican II brought some fresh and conciliatory statements from the Catholic church, insisting on the universal priesthood of all believers. But the differences between the laity and the ordained ministry still remained, not just in terms of function and degree, but also in 'essence' or 'nature'.[11] However, the whole concept of an 'ontological change' is being questioned, even amongst Catholics.

[1] Kung op. cit. pp.37ff.
[2] R Hanson Christian Priesthood Examined (Lutterworth, 1979) p.41.
[3] C Eastwood, The Priesthood of All Believers (Epworth, 1960) p. xii.
[4] A Richardson (ed.) Dictionary of Christian Theology (SCM, 1969) p.188.
[5] Hanson op. cit pp.81,82.
[6] Op. cit. p.64.
[7] Ibid. p. 90.
[8] Richardson op. cit. p.188.
[9] BMU The Priesthood of the Ordained Ministry (GS 694) p.7.
[10] M Thurian op. cit. pp.126f.
[11] D Wright, 'Ministry and Priesthood' Anvil, III 3, (1986) p.197.

In current ecumenical debate, the WCC Faith & Order Paper 116 con-fidently states, in relation to ministerial priesthood, that 'a convergence is beginning to emerge which would have been inconceivable even a few years ago'.[1] There have certainly been misunderstandings in the use of terminology which are now being overcome. However, professional theologians engaged in ecumenical debate often forget that what they might understand may be very different from what the average Christian may infer, both from terminology and from ritual.

Misinterpretation is not just in terms of words, but of vestments, titles, liturgy, ritual, training etc.. Doctrine is not simply deposited on library shelves! BEM was at pains to point out that such ministry 'has no exist-ence apart from the community' and that it is not 'exclusive' (p.22). However, it is clearly the case that presbyters do have an exclusive function—namely celebration of the eucharist (plus blessing and absolu-tion, which are intimately connected with it).

It is particularly worth looking at the conclusions of Hanson and the BMU report, since they represent an Anglican contribution to the debate. Han-son suggests that ordained priests 'stand for God to their fellow men and represent their fellow men to God' (p.100). 'Essentially a go between person' (p.102). Thus if the eucharist is not celebrated by an ordained priest 'nobody can be sure that God will respond to the church's prayers and bless the elements' (p.109). In line with Hanson, the BMU report states[2] that 'Christian tradition uses the term priesthood to refer to:
i. the unique priesthood of Christ ii. the priesthood of the whole church iii. the ministerial priesthood of bishops and presbyters'.

(The last 'particularly in relation to the Eucharist' p.100). It concludes (p.101) that only in the new heaven and earth there will be 'no more need for sacraments or priests to mediate God's presence'. These statements deserve some comment:
i. 'Christian Tradition' is a difficult term, since it is open to very different interpretations. The step from the priesthoods of Christ and all believers, to 'ministerial priesthood' is without scriptural justification and is not per-suasively argued theologically. It is thus a shaky basis for unity, however desirable this might be. Wright argues that the priesthood of the ordained ministry is part of the priesthood of all believers, not a separate catagory.[3] It is worth pointing out that it is not necessary to hold a view of a separate ministerial priesthood in order to maintain a high view of the Eucharist, since, as BEM affirms, it is Christ who invites us to His meal at which He himself presides. This may serve to explain the significant number of High Churchmen and Roman Catholics who support lay presidency.
ii. It is not possible here to speak in detail about a theology of the Eucharist, but Hanson's statement about whether God will respond to prayer and bless the elements focuses once again the attention on the status of the priest rather than on the celebration as an act of the whole community which he represents. If Selwyn is correct in detecting

---

[1] *Ibid.* p.127.
[2] BMU *op. cit.* p.97; also BEM *op. cit.* p.23 17.
[3] *Op. cit.* p.206.

'eucharistic overtones' in his commentary on 1 Pet. 2.5, it is striking that it comes in a passage most explicit, not about a special 'ministerial priesthood', but about the priesthood of all believers[1].

iii. Following on from the above, one might ask, if it is true that our assurance of God's response to prayer and blessing is dependent on the ordained priest, why do we allow deacons, and even lay people, to baptize, which, according to Luther 'consecrates us all . . . priests'. There appears to be a grave inconsistency in the church's practice and, by implication, in its theology.

iv. Finally, and perhaps most importantly, the concept of the ordained priest as a 'go between' whose 'mediation' would finally be unnecessary in heaven is in danger of reinforcing the concept of a special priestly class. How can we affirm that Christ is the only mediator and advocate, but then say that that access in the central point of our common life, the eucharist, must be mediated exclusivley through a special category of people? If I understand it correctly, this is what the diocese of Chile is concerned about when it refers to the 'priesthood of all believers'. It wants to affirm the ordained ministry as a focus for unity , order, sound doctrine, pastoral care and mission, without diminishing the wonder of direct access to God's grace through Christ for all believers—a principle which lies at the heart of our faith.

'Priest', 'mediator' and 'go between' are emotive terms theologically. It may be preferable to seek less ambiguous words. By 'mediator' Hanson seems to mean something nearer to the prophet who speaks for God and prays to God for the people. There are at least two ways of seeing a 'mediator'—as someone who stands in the way and restricts access except through himself, or as someone who brings parties together and facilitates their direct relationship with each other. The former marks an abuse of priesthood not unknown in the history of the church (and still common in South America). The latter we would wish to affirm. Yet we are left with the question, why can a lay person 'mediate' Christ in preaching, baptism, pastoral care, etc, yet not in the eucharist? I, at least, have not yet found a satisfying answer.

Ecclesiology
Let us look more briefly at what constitutes the church. We have already pointed to the growing body of opinion which begins its ecclesiology in the local Christian community, and intimately links presidency of the community with presidency at the eucharist. We have also noted that the eucharist is central to the life of such a community and pointed out that wheras the ordained ministry as we know it is not of the essence of the church, the eucharist certainly is. The question then arises, how does such a community form part of the universal church? In practice there are many ways in which denominations have developed this link, though all are imperfect, for the church continues to be divided. As we have observed, no single structure can be adequately demonstrated from Scripture.

The majority of Christians continue to accept the three-fold ordained ministry as the concrete way in which unity is maintained. Such is the case in the Anglican Communion. However, as Cobb pointed out in his letter to

[1] E. Selwyn *The 1st Epistle of St Peter* (Macmillan, 1946) pp.157f.

the Provincial Council, drawing a parallel with the doctrine of the Trinity, historically the issue of substance became more important than relationships. Thus, in the ordained ministry we see developing historically a great deal of emphasis on the status of the minister, whether an ontological change takes place, and what happens when hands are laid on an ordinand with the invocation of the Spirit, rather than the relationships that are being entered into or confirmed, between the local community on the one hand, and the wider church, represented by the bishop, on the other. For the presbyter, it is surely the communion he enjoys with, and which is officially recognized by, both parties which provides the basis for his authority, which is not separate from his responsibility to both. (Note that this assumes a strong relationship between local church and bishop which is not always evident in the Church of England, but which, for various reasons, does exist in the Cono Sur.) Thus to describe an ordained minister as a 'focus of unity' would certainly be correct in these terms.

Such a view precludes the use of the reserved sacrament or of travelling 'mass' priests as an adequate means of providing local eucharistic celebrations. The first depends too heavily upon a particular 'ontological' understanding of priesthood and eucharist, as well as undermining the concept of eucharistic celebration as a single act. Both divorce authority from responsibility and relationship.

Where then does that leave lay presidency? As we have already seen, there exist numerous situations where leadership exists in a local community, which is desirous of full fellowship with the wider church, and which accepts the Bishop's authority, but where it seems right to allow time to test whether a person is being called into the ordained ministry (in the traditional view, an irreversible step, constituting a life long calling). There seems then to be an irreconcilable problem. The local community cannot fully express its life without the eucharist, yet it has no one to preside at its celebrations. Is there any solution?

The question was earlier asked: what is the difference between delegation (via an episcopal licence) and ordination? It deserves a satisfying answer. The BMU[1] sees licensing as the joint recognition of a person by community and bishop for a particular work in a local church, wheras ordination is 'authoritative service' in the 'universal church'. By implication the former is temporary, since it involves no indefinite commitment to the locality, wheras the latter is permanent. (Though in fact, for an ordained minister in the Anglican church, a licence is still necessary in order to function in a particular locality.)

Hence, it seems perfectly acceptable that a person should be ordained, where there is confirmation of a lifelong calling and the equipping for the task, and that such an ordination be carried out by the Bishop, as representing the universal church, with the laying on of hands, symbolizing not only the passing on of authority but the invocation of the Spirit for grace for the task. (No one would deny that the ordinand is ultimately entirely dependent on God's grace to fulfil his ministry.) Nor is this separate from the local church, since it is always in the context of a calling to serve in a particular community.

[1] BMU, GS 281, para.19.

However, where the conditions for ordination are not met, and where a community is without an ordained minister, though not without leadership, it would seem perfectly reasonable that the bishop, in agreement with the community, should delegate his authority to a lay person in the form of a licence, for a specific task in the one local community and for a definite period. Universality would be maintained because the community would be in fellowship with the bishop through the licensed the lay leader, who would provide an adequate focus of unity at the Eucharist. (This is a very different situation from someone presiding without authorization, and much preferable to the development of 'ad hoc' leadership.) Accordingly a high view of the Eucharist and of order and universality could all be maintained. Even the indelibility of orders could be maintained, though it would not automatically imply an exclusive right or power to celebrate the Eucharist in any situation, since that belongs firmly within the Christian community, not with the ordained minister.

Going back to an earlier point, it may then be preferable to call this 'delegated presidency'. We may even find ourselves agreeing with the Methodists that this constitutes temporary ordination. Whether we do or not, it is high time some serious thought was given to the whole issue of indelibility of orders.

We are still left with some anomalies. Firstly, the Deacon and Reader do not find a place in such a scheme. Currently, in practice at least, both are effectively only separated from the priesthood by 'the ability to say one prayer at the Communion service'.[1] It would surely be better to combine the two into a single category and see them as assistants to the priest— but that is a different (though not unrelated) issue, for which the HUMA document might again provide a useful starting point. Where there were no priest, they could be licenced to preside at Holy Communion.

Secondly, what of home groups, houseparties etc. who wish to celebrate the eucharist, but where there is no priest? One could argue, again citing Ignatius of Antioch[2], that delegation of authority does not end with the bishop, but can be rightly used within the congregation by its president to authorize others to preside. This would maintain order and the link with the universal church, but it is, perhaps, taking the argument too far, and openning the door to abuse. Presbyterial presidency has been 'surprisingly effective in keeping the eucharist as the act of the church rather than the preserve of some zealous or entrepreneurial group or leader'.[3] It is therefore the more important to stress the stringent controls proposed in HUMA for lay presidency, as well as for other expressions of leadership, such as preaching and leading worship, which are no longer the unique preserve of the priest.

The Question of Method
Stephen Sykes, seeking to defend and uphold the 'Integrity of Anglicanism', speaks of 'the existence of a discernible Anglican standpoint emerging from its liturgy and canon law'.[4] However, his case appears to be

[1] Lloyd op. cit. p.14.
[2] ARCIC op. cit. para.12; God's Reign and Our Unity, op. cit. para.81.
[3] M Vasey, Personal Communication 2 May, 1990.
[4] S. Sykes The Integrity of Anglicanism (Mowbrays, 1978) p.74.

steadily crumbling, with the growing pace of liturgical reform and dramatic differences in canon law throughout the Communion (eg. women bishops in ECUSA whilst some Provinces will not contemplate ordaining women deacons). If theological grounds are appealed to, the differences are even more stark, with the likes of Tony Higton and Don Cupitt uneasily co-existing within the same Province. Is there, then, any common ground on which to build together? We have already noted the lack of cohesion of the arguments in HUMA. Most other denominations would provide us with a systematic framework at least as a basis for engaging in debate. However, we are increasingly hard pressed to find such a point of reference within Anglicanism today.

Although we may lament this, we may also rejoice in it. For the fact is that despite all their differences, Anglicans of many different persuasions have managed to remain in communion with each other. Despite the difficulties of debate at Lambeth, bishops experienced the joy of fellowship and worship together and strengthened their ties with each other. Disputes remained as disputes within the family. This is surely the glory of Anglicanism, the ability to accomodate many different traditions within the one church—a sort of mini-ecumenical project within itself. Though there are many difficulties, its treasure is in its very diversity.

As stated earlier, growing ecumenical dialogue, convergence on essentials and hopes of concrete steps towards unity mean a commitment to diversity (almost certainly including full communion with some denominations which already accept 'lay presidency'), rather than uniformity. It seems to reflect the old maxim:
> Firm on fundamentals
> Flexible on secondaries
> Charitable in all things.

If Anglicans can contemplate such an eventuality, hopefully they will be generous enough to contemplate lay presidency within their own communion as well.

For those who still find the thought unpalatable, perhaps they would care to demonstrate theologically the essential link between presidency of Holy Communion and ministerial priesthood, given that baptisms, preaching and teaching (which many would regard as potentially more damaging to unity than eucharistic presidency), as well as other areas of ministry, are regularly undertaken by deacons and lay people. They might also wish to defend the concept of 'indelibility of orders', which, if relaxed, could provide another way forward for those seeking to ensure regular provision of communion to all the faithful. There is no desire here to threaten further our unity, but to provide satisfactory solutions to real and pressing needs within the church from the 'springs of living water' which have been entrusted to us.